WILLIAM BOLCOM

BIRD SPIRITS

Nine Piano Pieces

Crows by
Frank Boyden

Bird Spirits is recorded on the Centaur Records CD [CRC 2953], *multiplicities: '38*, by Blair McMillen.

ISBN 978-1-4584-1691-9

EDWARD B. Marks music COMPANY

EXCLUSIVELY DISTRIBUTED BY
HAL•LEONARD® CORPORATION
7777 W. BLUEMOUND RD. P.O. BOX 13819 MILWAUKEE, WI 53213

www.ebmarks.com
www.halleonard.com

NOTE ON THE MUSIC

In 1999, Frank Boyden asked me for a piano piece to give his wife, Jane, for her retirement and asked how much I'd charge. I didn't want to ask for money but requested some piece of Frank's art in exchange, whereupon he sent me a beautiful set of drypoints of crows. They became the impetus for my work; each page of music, facing a crow print, reflects the mood of each bird-attitude, so that their visual message can influence the musical interpretation of each Bird Spirit.

—William Bolcom

NOTES ON THE PRINTS

During the winter of 1995, I spent hours feeding and drawing crows in a Safeway parking lot. The birds were very close and very active. I was fascinated by the incredible complexity of their movements and the exaggerated contortions of their bodies as they interacted. I produced many drawings and drypoints, of which I selected nine. I produced nine prints each in an edition of thirty. This suite was titled *Stances*. The original prints are printed with a very faint tan background. As I did not wish to duplicate the first edition, the prints in this book are black and white.

—Frank Boyden

CONTENTS

Page

I. **Bold and bright** 3

II. **Light and smooth, with gentle accentuation** 5

III. **Implacable** 7

IV. **Dignified** 8

V. **Quasi alla marcia** 11

VI. **Preparing for a long flight** 13

VII. **Ferociously** 14

VIII. **Stately, sustained** 17

IX. **Simply, very strong and forceful, yet lyrical** 18

for Jane Boyden

BIRD SPIRITS

I.

William Bolcom
(1999)

Bold and bright (♩ = 63)

9/24/99
Chicago

II.

Light and smooth (♩. = 76), with gentle accentuation

u.c., almost no **Ped.**

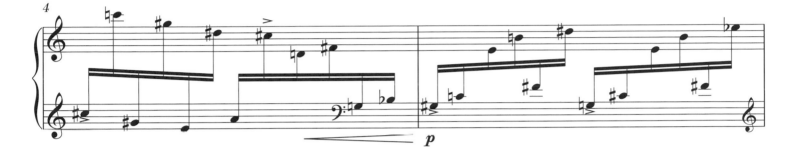

non rit.

9/25/99
Chicago

III.

Implacable (♪ = 116), (slight accents)

9/28/99
Chicago

IV.

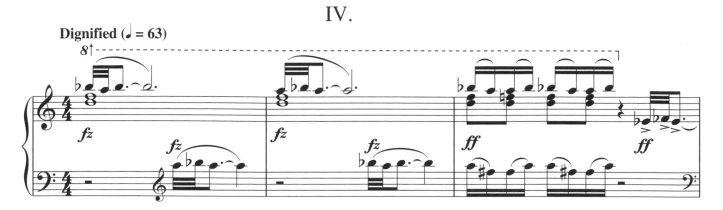

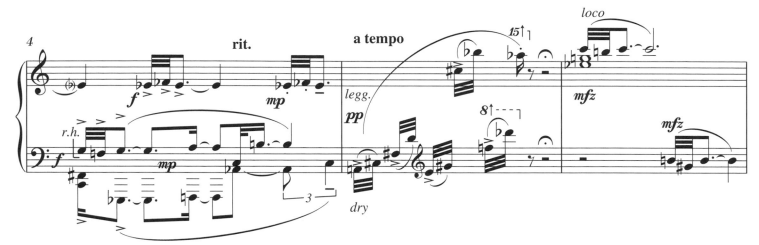

10/16/99
Ann Arbor

V.

11/22/99
Ann Arbor

VI.

Preparing for a long flight (♩ = 108); <u>not too fast</u>

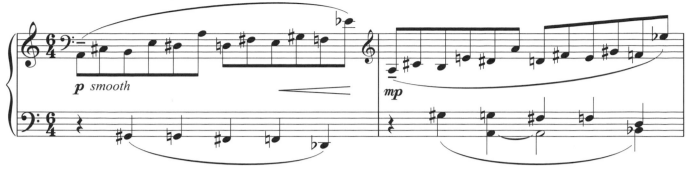

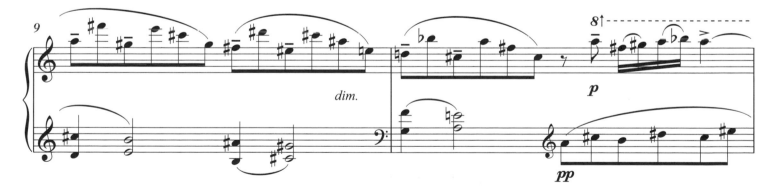

2/5/00
Ann Arbor

VII.

Ferociously (𝅝 = 88)

NB: accent changes

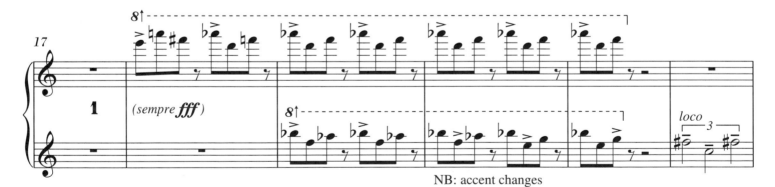

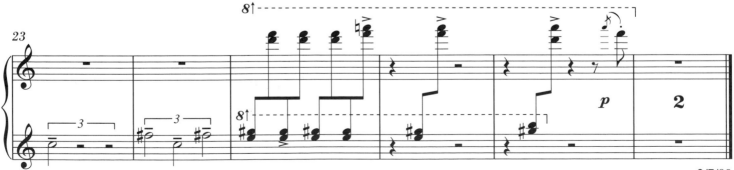

2/7/00
Ann Arbor

VIII.

Stately (♩ = c. 48), sustained

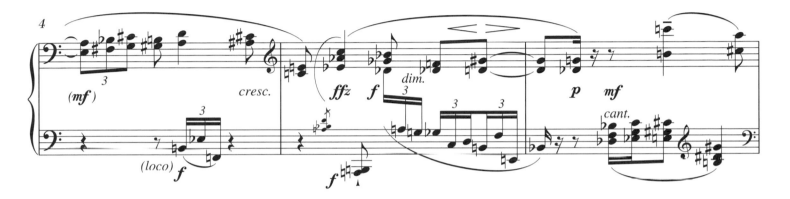

Upper 2 staves: hold till silent, release S.P.

2/7/00
Ann Arbor

IX.

Simply, very strong and forceful, yet lyrical (♩ = 58)

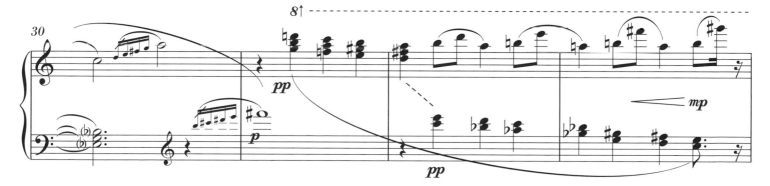

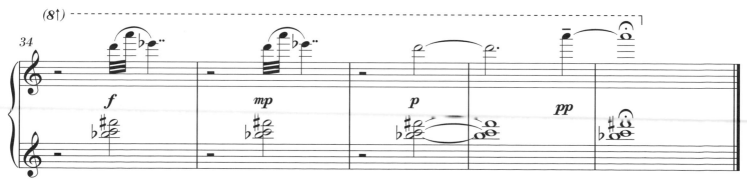